Clouds

A Compare and Contrast Book

by Katharine Hall

Some clouds are big and fluffy;

others are thin and wispy.

Some clouds are colorful;

others are dark with rain.

Some clouds tell us a storm is coming;

or that a storm has passed.

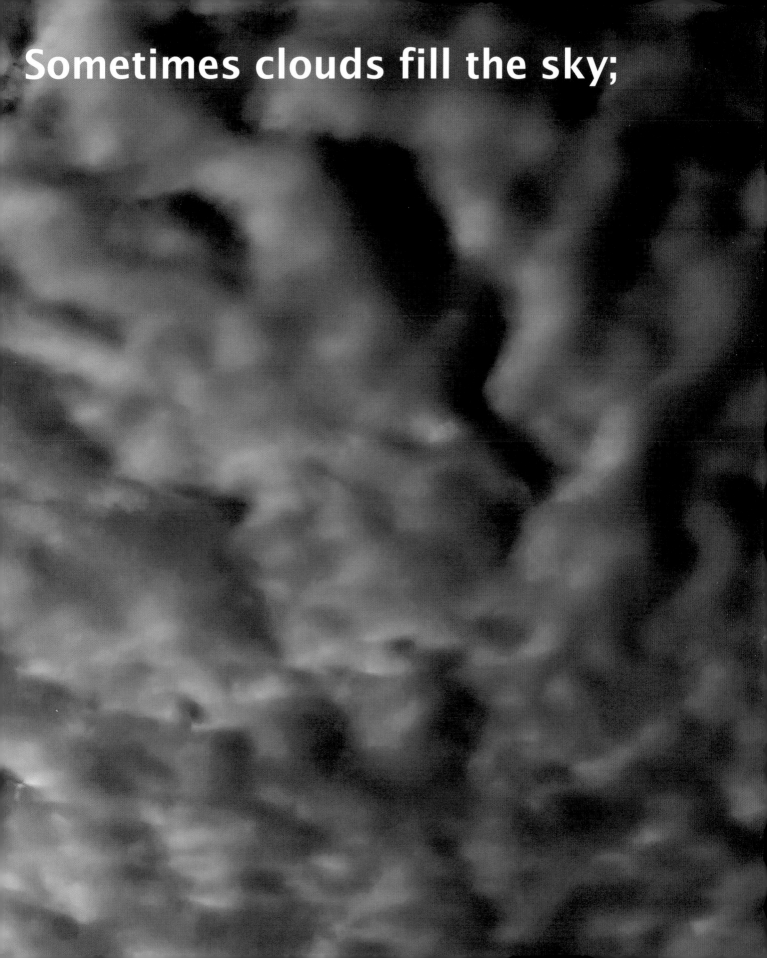

Sometimes clouds fill the sky;

but other times there are
no clouds in the sky.

Some clouds are on the ground;

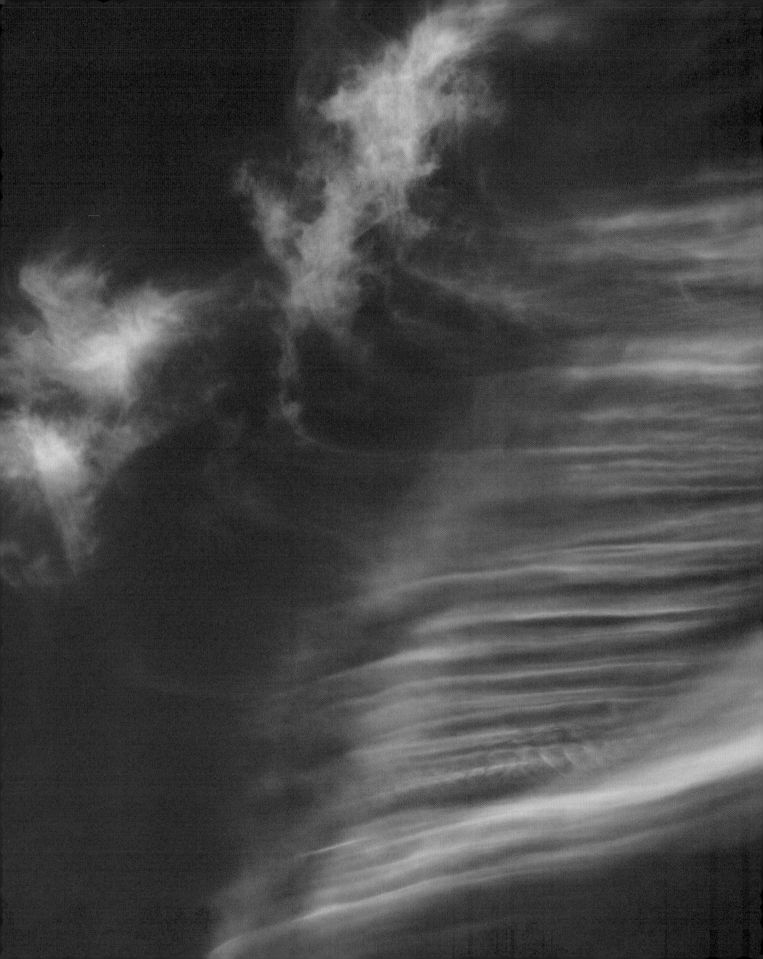

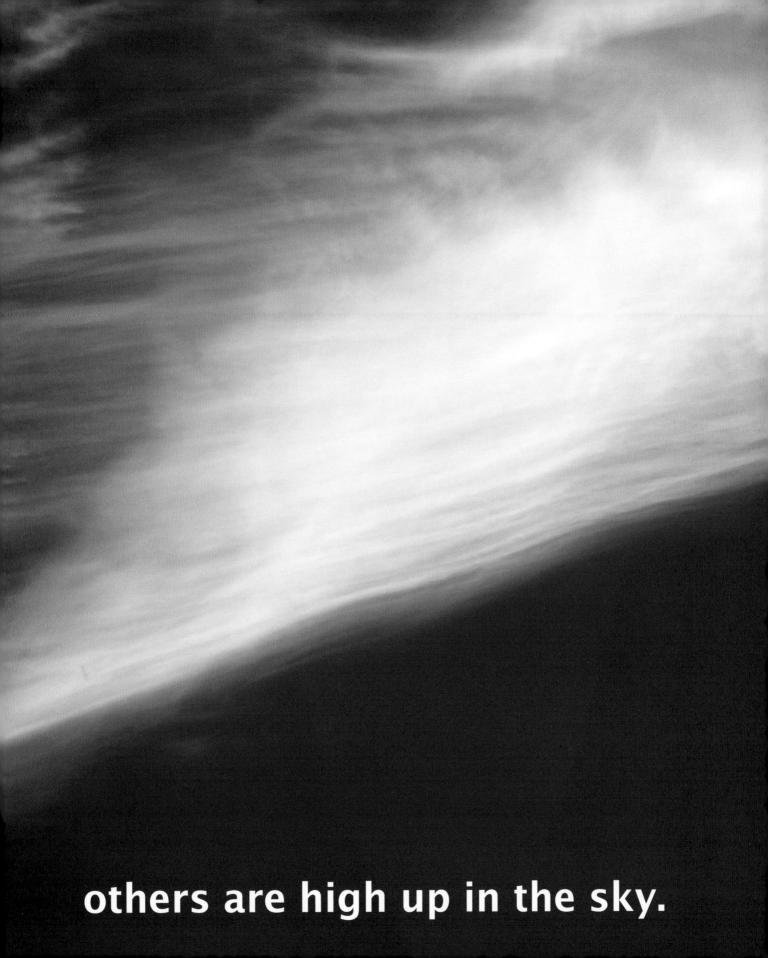

others are high up in the sky.

Some clouds swirl;

and others blanket the sky.

Clouds are all around us.

For Creative Minds

What are Clouds?

Clouds are collections of small water droplets or ice crystals floating in the atmosphere. They are made as part of the water cycle. There are three major stages to the water cycle:

1. **Evaporation:** When water gets hot enough, it turns into vapor (steam) and rises into the air. This occurs naturally when the sun heats the surface of a body of water. If you have ever seen a pot of water boiling on the stove, you've seen evaporation!

2. **Condensation:** When water vapor cools in the atmosphere, it changes from vapor into tiny droplets of water, or even ice crystals in very cold air. These water particles gather together and form clouds.

3. **Precipitation:** When so much water has gathered in a cloud that it is heavier than the air around it, the water falls back to the ground as precipitation. There are many different kinds of precipitation, including rain, hail, sleet, and snow.

Water Cycle Experiments

See evaporation in action

Materials: You will need a plastic cup, a marker, and water.

Process: Fill the cup halfway with water. Use the marker to indicate the top surface of the water. Leave the cup in the sunlight for several hours or for a whole day.

Observe: How has the water level in the cup changed?

Results: There is less water in the cup now then there was before. Some of the water in your cup evaporated.

See condensation in action

Materials: You will need a glass cup and ice.

Process: Fill the glass cup with ice and leave it on a table for at least twenty minutes.

Observe: When you come back, what do you notice on the outside of the glass or on the table underneath the cup?

Results: The water on the outside of the glass or under the cup did not leak through the cup—it came from the air! The ice in the glass caused the glass and the air nearby to cool. Water in the air changed from vapor to liquid, and clung to the surface of the cup or table. The cooler temperature created by the ice caused condensation.

See precipitation in action

Materials: You will need a ceramic mug, plastic wrap, a large bowl at least five to six inches deep, and a rubber band large enough to stretch around the bowl.

Process: Fill the bowl with 1-2 inches of water. Place the empty ceramic mug in the center of the bowl. Cover the bowl with plastic wrap and use the rubber band to hold the plastic wrap in place. Leave the bowl in the sunlight all day and let it sit overnight.

Observe: When you come back, what can you observe about the plastic wrap? Is it wet or dry? Is there anything inside the ceramic mug? Is the inside of the mug wet or dry?

Results: The entire water cycle has taken place within your bowl! First the heat from the sun caused evaporation from the water in the bowl. Next, the water vapor gathered at the top of the bowl, just under the plastic wrap. During this condensation, it formed small droplets that clung to the plastic surface. Finally, the droplets grew larger and heavier until they fell. This precipitation rained down into the ceramic mug and back into the water in the bowl.

Match the Clouds

There are four major categories of clouds: cirrus, cumulus, stratus, and nimbus. Use the following descriptions to identify the cloud types shown below. There are two of each of the following three kinds of cloud.

A. Wispy clouds with a white or light gray color are **cirrus** clouds.

B. **Cumulus** clouds look like a heap of puffy cotton balls.

C. **Stratus** clouds are flat and hazy. Stratus clouds sometimes cover much of the sky and can form as low-lying, misty fog.

Bonus: A **nimbus** cloud is any cloud that produces precipitation. They are usually dark gray and can be combined with other kinds of clouds. A cumulus cloud that produces precipitation is called a cumulonimbus. Can you identify the cumulonimbus on this page?

1.

2.

3.

4.

5.

6.

Weather Predictions

Clouds can be used to predict the weather.

A few **cirrus** clouds are a sign of clear weather, but a large group of cirrus clouds indicates that the weather will change within 24-36 hours.

When **cumulus** clouds are white, puffy, and spread out in a single horizontal layer, they are a sign of fair weather. When they pile up into vertical stacks and turn gray, cumulus clouds turn into cumulonimbus clouds. Cumulonimbus clouds can bring short bursts of heavy precipitation, lightning storms, high winds, or tornados.

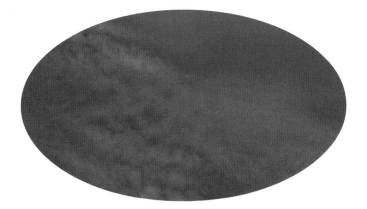

Stratus clouds often gather in thick blankets that cover much of the sky. When they form overnight, they generally disappear in the morning, leaving clear weather for the rest of the day. Precipitation from nimbostratus clouds is generally light rain, mist or snow flurries, but can last for several days.

Any cloud that produces precipitation is a nimbus cloud. Nimbus clouds are dark gray and a clear sign that precipitation is coming. A stratus cloud that produces precipitation, like this misty fog, is a nimbostratus.

To my parents, Donna and Lee, who taught my sisters and me to collect atmospheric data and record our observations so that we would be able to better predict the weather—KH

Thanks to Dave Williams, Chief Meteorologist with ABC News 4 (Charleston, SC), for verifying the accuracy of the information in this book.

Library of Congress Cataloging-in-Publication Data

Hall, Katharine, 1989-
  Clouds : a compare and contrast book / by Katharine Hall.
      pages cm. -- (Compare and contrast books)
  ISBN 978-1-62855-449-6 (english hardcover) -- ISBN 978-1-62855-457-1 (english pbk.) -- ISBN 978-1-62855-473-1 (english downloadable ebook) -- ISBN 978-1-62855-489-2 (english interactive dual-language ebook) -- ISBN 978-1-62855-465-6 (spanish pbk.) -- ISBN 978-1-62855-481-6 (spanish downloadable ebook) -- ISBN 978-1-62855-497-7 (spanish interactive dual-language ebook) 1. Clouds--Juvenile literature. I. Title.
  QC921.35.H35 2014
  551.57'6--dc23
                              2014011144

Translated into Spanish: Nubes: un libro de comparación y contraste

Lexile® Level: 230
key phrases for educators: clouds, compare/contrast, weather

                              Bibliography:
"Cloud Classification and Characteristics." National Oceanic and Atmospheric Administration (July 2, 2011). Accessed
        December 2013. <http://www.crh.noaa.gov/lmk/?n=cloud_classification>.
"Cloud Types." Department of Atmospheric Sciences at the University of Illinois at Urbana-Champaign. Accessed January
        2014. <http://ww2010.atmos.uiuc.edu/%28Gh%29/guides/mtr/cld/cldtyp/home.rxml>.
"How to Predict the Weather using Clouds." Section Hiker: Hiking and Backpacking for Beginners and Experts (October 13,
        2008). Accessed January 2014. <http://sectionhiker.com/predicting-the-weather-using-clouds>.

Thanks to Terry Hall for the use of his photograph for this book, and to the remaining photographers for releasing their images into the public domain.

Photograph:	Source:
Cover	Lisa Runnels
Titlepage	Ronald Carlson
Summer Clouds	Bobbi Jones Jones
Wispy clouds	Mark Calzaretta
Sunrise and Trees	George Hodan
Stormy Weather over Florida	Alex Grichenko
Tropical Storm is Coming	Petr Kratochvil
Summer Rainbow over Open Field	Barb Ver Sluis
Morning Sky	George Hodan
Sea Surface with a Wave	Petr Kratochvil
Fog	George Hodan
Blue Sky with Clouds	Petr Kratochvil
Roped Out tornado visible in distance	NOAA's National Severe Storm's Laboratory
Bold White Cumulus Clouds	Lynn Greyling
Clouds Stormy and Bright	Bobbi Jones Jones
Beautiful Clouds	Larisa Koshkina
Low cloud on the volcanic cliffs	Dr. James P. McVey, NOAA
Cirrus and Evergreens	Terry Hall

Manufactured in China, November 2014
This product conforms to CPSIA 2008
First Printing

Arbordale Publishing
Mt. Pleasant, SC 29464
www.ArbordalePublishing.com